IMAGES
of America

WEST
LONG BRANCH

IMAGES
of America

WEST
LONG BRANCH

Helen-Chantal Pike

ARCADIA

First published 1996
Copyright © Helen-Chantal Pike, 1996

ISBN 0-7524-0472-5

Published by Arcadia Publishing,
an imprint of the Chalford Publishing Corporation
One Washington Center, Dover, New Hampshire 03820
Printed in Great Britain

Library of Congress Cataloging-in-Publication Data applied for

*This book is dedicated to Charles Hulick Maps Jr., Meps descendent,
fellow photographer, adventurer through Jersey Shore history,
and gentle and generous friend.*

Contents

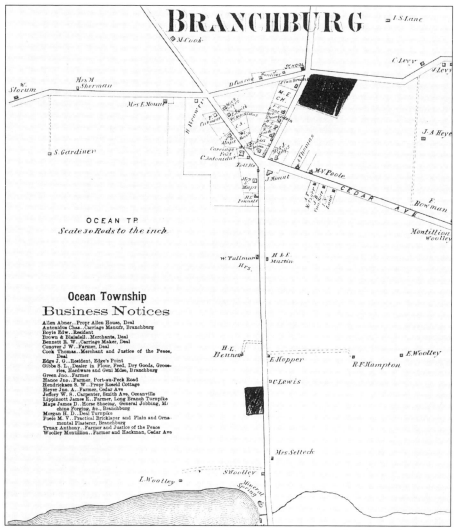

The area today known as West Long Branch was historically included in four successive township governments before achieving its independence. It was first part of Shrewsbury, the successor to the original colonial land grant known as the Monmouth Patent, and became part of Ocean in 1849. The short-lived political division of Lincoln (located along Locust Avenue and Wall Street) contained West Long Branch beginning in 1867, and Eatontown controlled the area, along with Oceanport, in 1873.

In May 1904 Long Branch City's boundary lines were finally adopted, resulting in a split of the city's upper village with Eatontown Township along Norwood and Oakwood Avenues, Broadway, and Wardell's Creek (which empties into Turtle Mill Brook). The tiny colonial stagecoach stop began with the name of Branchburg as it related to Branchport Creek, the nearby lower branch of the South Shrewsbury River, where docks for trade and travel were located. The South Shrewsbury is fed by Turtle Mill Brook, among others.

In 1815 West Long Branch was known as Hoppertown after New Yorker John Hopper, who bought the colonial inn. By 1865 it was called Mechanicsville because of the residents there who practiced that trade. But the name switched back to Branchburg to avoid confusion with another New Jersey town by the same name.

The two black squares in this 1873 Beers Atlas are the Methodist cemeteries.

6

Introduction

May 5, 1908, dawned as a busy day in West Long Branch. Civic leaders, lead by Munroe V. Poole, a local mason contractor, would work from early morning to dusk to get voters to the ballot box. At stake was nothing less than secession from Eatontown Township.

When this century began, West Long Branch was already a well-to-do community. Wealthy New Yorkers from the retail, brokerage, and entertainment industries built country cottages the size of mansions along its eastern border nearest to Long Branch, the resort capitol of the Jersey Shore. Most of the farmers and merchants prospered, in part, from servicing these large estates. This prosperity created a hefty—and not unenviable—tax base for which the year-round residents wanted their proportionate share of municipal services.

According to *The Advertiser*, an Eatontown newspaper at that time, prominent township residents countered this independence movement by driving their own cadre of voters to the community's polling station. The Eatontowners' intent was to drive more supporters to the poll throughout the day. But on the first trip, the car broke down, and it wasn't repaired until after the poll closed.

When the votes were tallied, the referendum passed 163 to 73. Among the first decisions made by the new mayor and council was to ask the Monmouth County Board of Freeholders for stone-paved roads on Cedar Avenue and Monmouth Road to replace the dusty dirt ones where, not coincidentally, the town's more affluent residents lived. A second request was for the installation of lights on Wall Street and Monmouth Road; a third was for for the widening of the increasingly trafficked Monmouth Road south from Wall Street.

Time passed. Commerce spread from the town's original colonial intersections. Tradesmen, many of immigrant descent, set up shops on and off Broadway in Kensington Park. A silk mill was built. Family-owned businesses flourished. A second firehouse was added. A larger, more modern elementary school was erected. Eventually a regional high school went up near a field where watercress once grew.

In 1942, the state laid an asphalt corridor—State Highway No. 36—through the green farmland south of Turtle Mill Brook to create a short-cut to the shore. Locally it is named Monmouth Park Highway for the racetrack that borders the town line in neighboring Oceanport. Gradually, farms gave way to suburban houses whose streets took their names from community leaders, and the borough designed a master plan that took modern industry into account.

As the next century appears on the horizon, West Long Branch still has a town-and-country identity. Those who live here affectionately call it *the borough* after its mayor-and-council form of government, and many men, and some women, still go by nicknames given to them in a bygone era when everyone knew everyone else.

There is still country in the town, horses to be found, and open, green land where farms once stood. Most striking is the social and economic relationship the town continues to have with its more famous country estates that are now the signature campus of Monmouth University.

Volume I of this planned two-volume set highlights the town's history. Volume II will hold the mirror up to its country visage.

Minutes from the June 22, 1908, council meeting that formally established the borough of West Long Branch. Arthur D. Van Note was appointed borough clerk; Fred A. Beale, tax assessor with an assessor's bond set at two hundred dollars; George L. Gibbs, tax collector; and George A. Hulick, superintendent of highways.

One
Begun by Referendum

The first mayor and council of West Long Branch. From left to right are: (front row) Council President Thomas W. Cooper Sr., Mayor Monroe V. Poole, Dr. Edward M. Beach (finance committee), and Frank S. Brand; (back row) Thaddeus Schenck, Charles A. Poole, and John H. Sutphen (both finance committee members).

In this view of Monmouth Road and Cedar Avenue *c.* 1900, a produce-wagon scale is in the center. Scotsman Alexander McGregor built the inn (by 1804) on the Manasquan-Branchport stage route. It had wide clapboards, brick walls, hand-hewn timbers, doweled beams, six fireplaces, and Dutch doors. When McGregor went home, he sold the inn and 40 acres to John Hopper. Dr. Beach's house is to the left.

John Short's House (left) and Carriage Manufactory appear on the west side of Monmouth Road, *c.* 1890. Blacksmith Frank Sherman is to the right. W.M. Golden Foot Furnishings was a general store at Cedar and Locust Avenues. Golden was also a Justice of the Peace who advertised: "If you're in a flurry, to marry in a hurry; You can get a souvenir, when you find me here."

This simple two-story, white-frame structure was the site of many historic beginnings. It was the first firehouse. In 1908, the newly independent borough council held its first meeting on the second floor. A small addition was home to the first aid squad.

Still later, the Shadow Lawn Building & Loan Association had its first headquarters here. The picture on the right, taken in the late 1920s, shows the Short-Cooper house behind the Christmas tree.

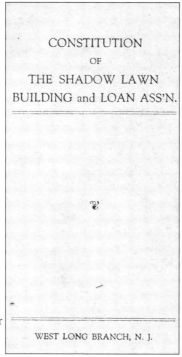

CONSTITUTION

OF

THE SHADOW LAWN
BUILDING and LOAN ASS'N.

WEST LONG BRANCH, N. J.

Frank Krug may have built W.M. Golden's store. Over time, the building housed a luncheonette, barbershop, pizzeria, beauty salon, and the post office. In the 1950s, American Stores Company, a forerunner to what was the Acme on Route 36 and Broadway, was here. The Jacobus House, left, had a small store, a gas pump, and, briefly, the public library, all on the ground floor.

This close-up shows the carriage shop that catered to the area's prosperous farmers and wealthy summer residents. Charles Antonides built carriages here in 1873. He was succeeded by John Short. Next door is Frank Sherman's horse-shoeing shop. This picture was taken c. 1890.

Monmouth Road heading south into the intersection from Wall Street. The Covert and Sherman homes are on the left. In the far distance is the McGregor House. The open lot on the left is part of the elementary school playground. This photograph was taken c. 1940.

By the turn of the century, Short's carriage factory business had given way to the repair and servicing of horseless carriages, and Tom Cooper Sr.'s family took over the enterprise. Alma Nichols's house, at right, is the Dot Schulze Real Estate Agency today.

Shown here from left to right are Harry, Dick, Jeanette, Marie, and Tom Cooper, grandchildren of Councilman Thomas Cooper Sr.

Dick and Harry lived in Short's house. Tom and his mother lived in the apartments over the garage, which was torn down in 1972 to make way for a modern Amoco station.

George L. Gibbs, who bought Walter Sherman's general store, stands with a mail pouch; he became the borough's first postmaster in 1897. He converted half the store for use as the post office, and let out the other half to the public library. Walking out of the photograph is Nellie Sherman, Frank's wife.

Monmouth Road looking south, late 1800s. The first farm on the left from the intersection was the Fulton Farm; on the right is the McGregor-Tallman House, commonly called the Cooper House.

The prosperous George Fulton Farm on Monmouth Road appears here between the current-day Woolley Place and Mount Drive.

The Fulton Farm is listed on the 1985 National Register of Historic Places; its oldest wing dates from 1737. Alexander McGregor owned it in 1790. William Tallman added the Greek Revival section in 1834. Tom Cooper Sr. bought the house in 1874. Great-grandson and Councilman Richard F. Cooper spent his childhood here. It was sold to Frances D. Wilson in 1946, to Hanmer W. Webb-Peploe in 1947, and to Borough Historian Nina Klein and her husband Gardner in 1954.

James Reynolds Mount is shown here with his mother Mary (seated), and oldest sister Lavenia (on the left). To Mount's right is Ella Isabelle Jeffrey, his wife. The little boy is Jim and Lavenia's nephew, George Van Huel, son of sister Phebe Mount Van Huel, who died in childbirth. Jim and Lavenia helped to raise their nephew George. A third sister, Susie, died at age twelve.

Mount was born June 10, 1861. Hardworking and thrifty, he began working at age nine with his father in local marl pits; he started farming at age fourteen. The Mounts farmed 47 acres in Poplar (the Oakhurst-Wayside section of Ocean between Routes 35 and 18), Wall Street (where Lavenia was born), and Monmouth Road. In the blizzard of 1888 he built this house for his father, mother, and sister.

17

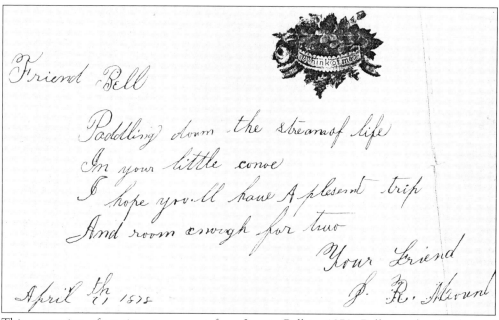

Friend Bell

Paddling down the stream of life
In your little canoe
I hope you'll have A plesent trip
And room enough for two

Your Friend
J. R. Mount

April 7th, 1878

This expression of sentiment was sent from Jim to Bell in 1878. Bell was the daughter of William Stewart Jeffrey, a local builder whose Elberon home would eventually be bought by a member of the Gimbels retail family of New York.

In 1895 Mount built an identical farmhouse for his bride-to-be, whom he married on January 1, 1896; the minister was Reverend Pennington Corson of Old First. The couple honeymooned by train, visiting New York, Baltimore, Richmond, and Washington. Bell moved in that spring. The house is now owned by Elsalyn Palmisano and Harris Drucker.

18

Jim's mother, Mary (above left), was one of three Reynolds sisters of Eatontown to marry into West Long Branch. Maccie W. married Charles A. Poole; Susie E. married Abram T. Metzgar. George Mount, originally from Manasquan, met his wife attending Sunday services in the Old First Church. Jim and Bell Mount are shown on the above right with a young Dot Dangler from Wayside, who came to live with and work for the Mounts when she was eighteen in 1908. Dot, the oldest in a large family, stayed with the Mounts until retiring at age seventy-five. She died in 1983 at age ninety-three.

The newlyweds are shown here in front of the barns on Monmouth Road. Bell died childless in 1925. She is buried in the Mount Crypt in Glenwood Cemetery. Mount was the cemetery association's president.

Mount in his carrot field. He sold his produce to Ulysses S. Grant, George W. Childs, and George Pullman. His 31-acre farm extended to Larchwood Avenue. Lavenia, who moved in after Bell's death, was his bookkeeper. After a small kitchen fire in Lavenia's original house, the building was torn down about 1960.

Mount had a dairy business and sold quarts of milk for 11¢; he apologized to his customers when industry laws forced him to raise the price to 13¢. As grocery stores grew into supermarkets, Mount gave up farming to landscape the summer estates. His specialty: private roadways, drives, and especially tennis courts.

Mount, a republican, launched a political career in 1913 with his election to the borough council. After seventeen years, he was appointed mayor when Mayor Samuel R. Baker died in March 1931 with ten months left in his term.

When Mount ran for the office, he was elected and became New Jersey's oldest and longest-running mayor. He was opposed only once, in 1934, and he defeated his democratic opponent 603 to 90.

During the Depression years, Mount and Council President Owen Woolley, who had a dental practice on Broadway in Long Branch, helped pay the borough's bills and teachers' salaries.

In this photograph Mount is being sworn in by his political protégé, Borough Clerk J. Russell Woolley (no immediate relation to Owen). The year is 1943—half-way through Mount's mayoral tenure.

In a 1950 interview Mount said: "I think West Long Branch has a great future and will expand to the fullest. I regret our last increase in the tax rate [$18], but I'm afraid we've been over-economizing for too many years . . . we've got to have schools and I'm in favor of our children getting the best education possible."

Mount was also chairman of the Long Branch Banking Company and the Shadow Lawn Savings & Loan.

Lavenia and Jim Mount are seen together here at Jim's eighty-fifth birthday party at Joseph's, a restaurant on Monmouth Road.

"Uncle Jim," as most people remember him today, died on August 18, 1953, at age ninety-two, having served thirty-nine years in office and missing only 6 of 678 consecutive council meetings. At his birthday party two months earlier Mount observed: "I was brought up the hard way and I worked hard. But I was never discouraged."

"Aunt Lavene," as she was known, never married but apparently did have a boyfriend who would peddle his bicycle down Monmouth Road from Eatontown every Sunday to spend the day with her. The man was a Van Schoick who lived on the corner of Broad Street and Kelly's Lane, taking care of his widowed mother. At least once the couple was discovered clutched in an embrace on the parlor sofa.

It was Lavenia who made sure the outhouse behind the first home Mount built was cleaned out the day before Halloween, to lessen the social embarrassment caused by the local boys who moved the tiny building to the Monmouth Road and Cedar Avenue intersection every Halloween night. Jim Mount would pay the boys 25¢ each to move it back the next day.

Lavenia died October 30, 1962. She was 102.

Just before the Civil War, Egbert Hopper bought the toll house on the Old Plank Road near Corlies Pond (today Deal Lake), and moved it to his farm on Monmouth Road. Over the years, various additions to the right of the original toll house were put on.

The Palmer Family gathered in front of their house and barn on Palmer Avenue in 1886. The house eventually burned down. Today the barn's architecture has been highly modernized.

An 1851 Jesse Lightfoot map lists this Monmouth Road property as being owned by H.L. Bennett. The original property extended halfway down West Palmer Avenue, and is believed to have been a watermelon farm. The house has been enlarged and remodeled.

Mayor Samuel R. Baker lived in this house on the southeast corner of Palmer Avenue and Monmouth Road. His house was built in 1846 on a parcel that once went all the way to Whale Pond Brook. It is the current home of Councilman John Paolantonio.

24

William Brinley, a miller, owned two key properties on Monmouth Road. In 1791, he deeded 1 acre for a church "free for the use of all ministers of the Gospel . . . and for the exclusive use of the Methodists . . . every other Sunday." He also deeded the surrounding land for a burial yard. Among the trustees were Peter Parker, a Monmouth Patentee descendent, and Frederick Maps, a furniture maker. The church was built on the southwest corner of Monmouth Road and West Palmer Avenue.

The Free Methodists as well as Presbyterians worshipped here. But in 1808, dissension splintered the Methodists. The cause of the split was multi-fold, but it came about, at least partially, in response to Reverend Zenas Conger's objections to a trustee clause that designated the Annual Conference beneficiary if a church property ceased to be in use.

In any event, Conger and his followers, who were dubbed Congerites, established the Independent Methodist Congregation. The Independents seem to have reached their peak in 1820, and merged with the Methodist Protestants in 1850.

But by 1845, Harriet Baker, the mayor's widow, had already bought the church and had it moved across the road where it was converted for use as a barn. It is pictured here in 1927. It is no longer standing.

The oldest cemetery in the borough is the final resting place for Brinley, who died in 1840 at age ninety. John Slocum was the first to be buried here in 1791. The last recorded burial was of William Van Note on November 21, 1895. There are 103 recorded burials here. On Memorial Day in 1977, Jane Raviel, left, and Anita Fornino unveiled a commemorative marker.

Brinley's other key property was his mill on Whale Pond Brook in Oceanville (now Oakhurst). There was also a mineral spring on the property. One of the Hoppers owned the mill in 1851.

Cedar Avenue looking west. At left was the home of George Gibbs; on the right is that of Richard Hughes, a Welsh-born landscape artist who laid out John McCall's ornamental gardens and wishing well. Hughes also laid out Scenic Drive in Atlantic Highlands. He married Annie Van Note, whose father, J.D., was a partner in Poole and Van Note, a decorating and painting business.

General store owner, postmaster, tax collector, and custodian of school monies, George L. Gibbs is shown here c. 1880. His home, just west of present-day Baker Drive, is next door to the home of J.D. Van Note.

In 1865, John Davison Van Note purchased land from Isaiah Lane's estate. In 1868, the Civil War veteran who was first mate on a supply schooner for the Union Army built this house. On April 19, 1913, while serving as mayor, Van Note died. He was seventy years old.

The J.D. Van Note Family gathered for supper in their dining room. Clockwise from the upper right is Mary Williams Van Note, J.D. Van Note (Mary's husband), Annie Van Note Hughes (the couple's daughter), Richard Hughes, and Rowland and Kenneth Hughes (the Hugheses' sons).

Nancy Marion Van Note, Reginald's daughter, aged three, is shown on the above left outside the house where she still lives with her husband, Arthur C. Herry, a Crum descendent. Their daughter, Leeann J., and son-in-law, Robert Arnts, lived in the Hugheses' house with daughter Alice Rose. Reginald Fred Van Note is shown on the above right at three months when he was christened at what was then called the Old First Methodist Episcopal Church. Reginald married Marion Cornelia Joste of Asbury Park.

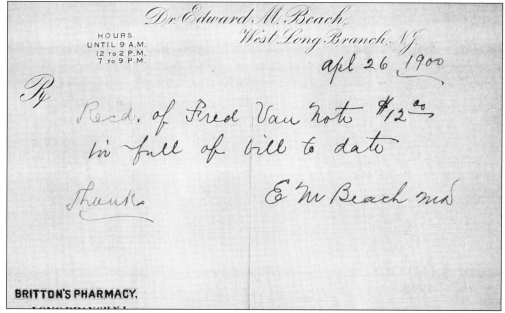

J.D. and Mary Van Note also had a son, Fred W., who was delivered by the Mississippi-born and University of Maryland-trained Dr. Edward Meeker Beach, who specialized in pediatrics. Fred followed his father's footsteps in the family business. He married Mary H. White of Oakhurst and had two children: Reginald F. and Alice E.

Emma Maps Thomas was born at 579 Cedar Avenue on August 4, 1876. Her father, Augustus, was a Civil War veteran. Emma went blind after contracting measles, and used a clothesline strung in the yard for navigation. Her house is on the north side of Cedar Avenue near Locust Avenue, two houses west of Monroe V. Poole's.

In 1873, according to the Beers Atlas, the Bowman family lived in this house. Daughter Josephine married Stewart Rich. Eleazer Collins Rich, Stewart's father, later lived in this house on the north side of Cedar Avenue. It was east of Monroe Street just after an open field on that corner, but is no longer standing.

The Hulick-Howland House, c. 1711, is probably the oldest standing structure in the borough at 496 Cedar Avenue. It is located on the south side, east of Larchwood Avenue.

This structure is identified only as the Harvey House on Cedar Avenue, although the Harveys may have lived first in the Maps House.

The 1873 Beers Atlas shows this building as the Julia Maps home on the corner where Locust and Cedar Avenues begin.

Frank and Charlotte Raab Krug bought the Mapses' house. In this turn-of-the-century photograph, Charlotte is the first on the left in the middle row, followed by her daughters Wilhelmina and Elizabeth, and George Van Huel (who married Elizabeth). Frank F. Krug was a carpenter who advertised "leaks a specialty." He is first on the right in the top row.

At left is the wedding announcement of Minnie Raab and "Brick" Woolley, a World War I sergeant major from Long Branch. Brick's childhood nickname was "Red" because of his hair color. He was one of nine children. The newlyweds lived in Dr. Beach's house.

Wooley worked for the New York and Long Branch Railroad at fourteen. He became West Long Branch borough clerk in 1921, and his first secretary was Gertrude Poole Bradley. His grandfather was Democratic Assemblyman William H. Bennett. From 1924-1929, the clerk's job was only part-time, so Wooley was also secretary to state senator William A. Stevens, the town's attorney. Wooley, renowned for his tenor voice, soled at the United Methodist Church in Red Bank.

Mr. and Mrs. Frank F. Krug

announce the marriage of their daughter

Wilhelmina Raab

to

Mr. John Russell Woolley

on Tuesday the twenty-fifth of December

nineteen hundred and seventeen

West Long Branch, New Jersey

This family get-together took place in the early 1930s. From left to right are: (front row) Frances and Doris Van Huel, and Virginia and John Russell "Chubby" Woolley Jr.; (back row) Frank Krug Jr., Charlotte and Frank Krug Sr., Brick and Minnie Woolley, and George and Elizabeth K. Van Huel.

THIRD ANNUAL

CLAMBAKE

Under the Auspices of the

444

REPUBLICAN CLUB

In Honor of

FREEHOLDER J. RUSSELL WOOLLEY

AT THE

MOOSE PARK, WAYSIDE, NEW JERSEY

SUNDAY, SEPTEMBER 10, 1939

Woolley's mother was a democrat, his father a republican. In 1936, when the republicans gained control of Monmouth County, Brick, a republican, was appointed clerk to the board of freeholders. Woolley became county republican chairman and acquired another nickname: Mr. Republican of Monmouth County.

For COUNTY CLERK

☒ J. RUSSELL WOOLLEY

J. RUSSELL WOOLLEY, candidate for county clerk to succeed the late Raymond L. Wyckoff, has been a member of the Board of Freeholders for three years, and previously served as clerk of the board. He has been in charge of the county highway department and has also directed the county's purchasing department.

He has been Borough Clerk in West Long Branch for 19 years, being appointed after he returned from active service with the A.E.F. in France during the World War. He is a past commander of the Long Branch post, American Legion.

He is a member of the Board of Education in his home town, a former fire chief, and a member of several fraternal orders.

In his political career, J. Russell was executive committee chairman of the state GOP and twice a delegate to national conventions. In a 1962 interview, Woolley said of his seven granddaughters, "I guess the good Lord thought there were enough people named Woolley, and that I didn't need any grandsons—in politics or out." Time would change that.

The West Long Branch Field Days, c. 1950, took place between Cedar Avenue and Wall Street. Mount's "sound judgment and counsel played a big part in my governmental activities," Woolley said in 1962.

J. Russell swears in Owen Woolley as mayor on September 3, 1953, following Mount's death. Since 1905 Woolley, born in Elberon, had lived on a Wall Street farm in West Long Branch. Dr. Woolley was first elected to office on April 2, 1931. Harry R. Vogel, planning board chairman, former Hillside mayor, and a Long Branch clothier, was appointed to Woolley's council seat.

Ella Giambrone's father, who worked on bridges for the county road department, set his daughter up with a farm on the northeast corner of Monmouth Road and Wall Street. Ella married John Herbert, a plumber. One of Ella's uncles was Joe Bilotta, who had a farm on the north end of Monmouth Road.

Stout Sherman, seen here c. 1900 on top of his hay wagon, farmed the northwest corner. Both corners are now parkland; Sherman's farm has already been developed and includes jogging paths, bicycle trails, and a composting site.

Slocum Farm, late 1800s. The Slocums—William and his two sisters, Charlotte and Ellen—had a huge strawberry field, and let customers pick their own for 2¢ a quart.

The Slocum property was eventually bought by John C. Giordano and named Windswept Farm. Giordano's 13.8 acres were gradually reduced to 3.8 acres as the surrounding land became a residential area. The farmhouse built for Giordano is now vacant.

The 1873 Beers Atlas shows this as the T. Eaton property; the house dates from 1844 and has been called Sandy Oaks. Big Band leader Arthur Pryor, who was living here at the time of his death in 1942, called it Driftwood. The Missouri native had two sons, Arthur Jr. and Roger, a movie star and later an advertising executive.

County Judge Giordano and J. Russell Woolley, *c.* 1940.

This 1956 aerial view shows Ray Croft, the Harold and John Disbrow brothers' chicken, feed, and farm supply business on Whale Pond Road. The little building in the trees to the right was the Cedar Sportsman Club house. The farm and house in the middle of the photograph belonged to Joseph Scarano, who bought it from Squire Chamberlain. Squire's daughter, Laura, married Dr. Edward Beach.

C. W. BRICK MILLING CO.

Cee-Bee ⟨B CEE E⟩ Feeds

Mills:
Columbus
Crosswicks
Flemington

Phone
Bordentown 635

COLUMBUS, N. J.

September 20, 1937

We offer, subject to our confirmation, for prompt delivery F. O. B.
Columbus or Flemington, N. J. Terms: Arrival Draft or Cash on delivery.
Your rail rate: Add___, Deduct___. Truck rate, 6 ton load___. E. & O. E.

CEE-BEE MANAMAR MASHES
100# Branded Cottons, Jutes $1.00 less.

*"S-G-L" (Starter-Grower-Layer)	49.95
*Starter and Broiler. . .	51.70
Poultry Fattener	48.95
Laying Mash.	50.20
Conditioner.	65.70
Turkey Starter	55.45
Turkey Grower.	49.70
Turkey Layer	52.20
Mash Concentrate	52.45

*50# Papers-Same: 25# Papers $1.00
10# Papers $4.50 higher.

CEE-BEE MASHES
100# Branded Jutes

Columbus Grower.	41.70
Columbus Laying Mash . .	44.20
Diamond Laying Mash. . .	41.70

(Cod Liver Oil in all mashes)

CEE-BEE MANAMAR DAIRY FEEDS
100# Branded Jutes

Calf Growing Feed. . . .	45.95
12% Fitting Ration . . .	38.95
19% Fitting Ration Concentrate	43.45
16% Dairy Feed	32.95
20% Dairy Feed	34.45
20% Super Dairy Feed . . .	
24% Dairy Feed	40.70
28% Supplemental	40.45
32% Concentrate.	44.95

CEE-BEE DAIRY FEEDS
100# Branded Jutes

11% Bulk Sweet Feed. . .	28.45
16% Dairy Feed	30.95
20% Dairy Feed	32.45
24% Super Dairy Feed . .	36.70
28% Supplemental	35.95
32% Concentrate. . . .	37.95
Columbus 24%	33.70

SCRATCH FEEDS
100# Branded Jutes

*CEE-BEE Scratch	42.95
COLUMBUS Scratch. . . .	41.45
COLUMBUS Inter Scratch. .	41.95
COLUMBUS Chick Scratch. .	51.20

*2nd Cottons 50¢ higher.
Papers - 50# $1.50: 25# $2.50:
10# $5.00 higher than Jutes

GRAINS
100# Sacks Included

Argentine Corn. . . .	40.95
Domestic Corn	46.20
*Cracked Corn - Argentine.	41.70
Pure Corn Meal. . . .	41.70
46# Barley	38.95
38# Clipped White Oats. .	32.70
Fine Grd. Oats.	32.95
Poultry Wheat	38.95

*Intermediate 50¢ more

INGREDIENTS

20% Alfalfa Leaf Meal .	42.70
Dried Brewers Grains. .	26.95
41% Cottonseed. . . .	32.20
Gluten Feed	31.95
34% O.P. Linseed Meal .	39.70
Flour Middlings - Clifton	33.95
41% Soybean Oil Meal. .	
Standard Bran	27.95

HORSE FEEDS & MISC.
100# Branded Jutes

CEE-BEE 14% Manamar Pig Feed.	43.20
CEE-BEE Horse Feed. . .	35.45
CEE-BEE 85% Horse Feed. .	41.95

The first price list used by John R. Disbrow.

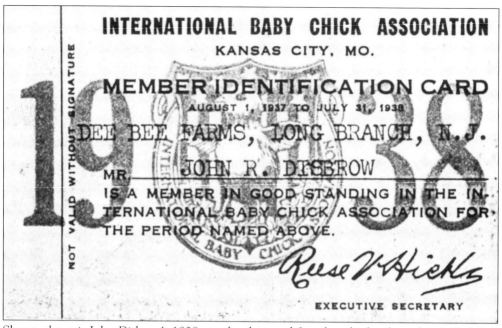

INTERNATIONAL BABY CHICK ASSOCIATION

KANSAS CITY, MO.

MEMBER IDENTIFICATION CARD

AUGUST 1, 1937 TO JULY 31, 1938

DEE BEE FARMS, LONG BRANCH, N. J.

MR. JOHN R. DISBROW

IS A MEMBER IN GOOD STANDING IN THE IN-
TERNATIONAL BABY CHICK ASSOCIATION FOR
THE PERIOD NAMED ABOVE.

Reese V. Hicks

EXECUTIVE SECRETARY

Shown above is John Disbrow's 1938 membership card for what the brothers then called Dee Bee Farms, an enterprise that included a large-scale incubator business for raising baby chicks.

Mr. and Mrs. Harold E. Disbrow appear together in May 1947.

The Disbrow farmhouse with a porch under construction by Harold Disbrow is shown here c. 1928.

View from the porch looking south. Whale Pond Road, the dividing line between West Long Branch and Eatontown, is at right.

A photographic copy of the indenture paper for Jurgh Michael Meps, who came from Rotterdam in 1754 to work for George Smith (who, in turn, came to Branchburg). The term of indenture lasted seven years. Meps married Smith's daughter, Barbara, bought his farm, and had a son, Frederick, who would grow up to work with him making furniture.

This ladder-backed chair has been attributed to Michael Meps. The photograph was taken in 1977 when the chair was owned by Edward King of Freehold.

Below is the Maps homestead located off Whale Pond Road. The "Meps" name evolved into "Maps." Michael Meps is buried in the Independent Methodists' graveyard on Monmouth Road.

Built in the early 1900s, 181 Wall Street was one of the first homes on the street to have city water. The old well is still in the basement.

Elijah and Catherine Worles built 171 Wall Street in the third quarter of the nineteenth century.

Number 167 Wall Street was built *c.* 1876 on that part of Lewis Lane's Locust Avenue farm that extended east to where the Mount Carmel Cemetery is today. It was moved in the early 1900s, perhaps in 1914, to make way for the Norwood Country Club golf course that once extended all the way to Oakwood Avenue.

Records from 1848 related to 141 Wall Street indicate this was known as the "Old Chinnery House."

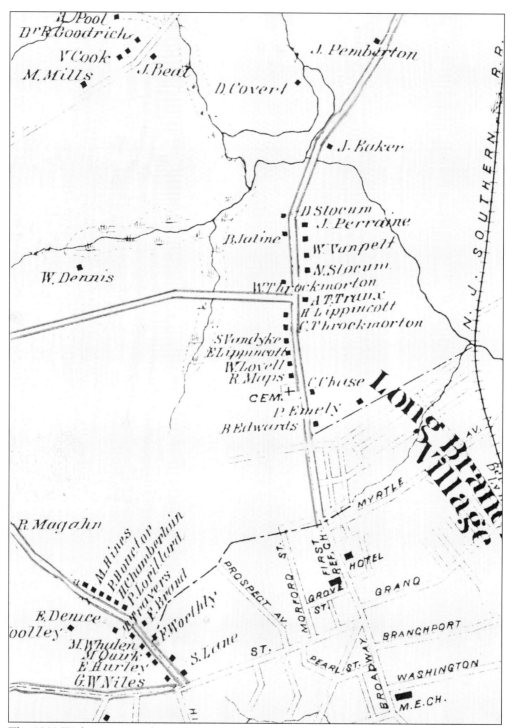

The 1889 Wolverton map shows Locust Avenue at Broadway. The creek flowing from Franklin Lake between the J. Baker and D. Slocum properties and under the railroad track empties into Pleasure Bay. The heavy dotted line shows the commonly-accepted boundary between Eatontown Township and Long Branch.

48

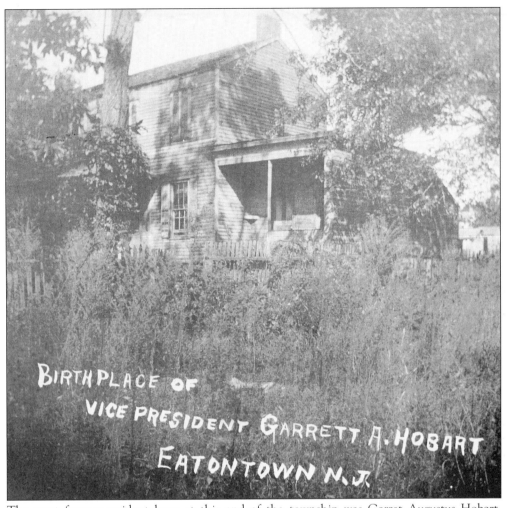

BIRTHPLACE OF VICE PRESIDENT GARRETT A. HOBART EATONTOWN N.J.

The most famous resident born at this end of the township was Garret Augustus Hobart, William McKinley's vice president. The pre-Revolutionary house he lived in was built on Broadway (today's North Locust Avenue) for Jacob Slocum.

In 1841, the house was leased to Addison W. Hobart of New Hampshire, who married Sophie Van Derveer of Marlboro and came to teach in Long Branch. Their son Garret was born in 1844. The family moved to Marlboro in 1852. Hobart, with a law degree, a wife, and a political office, eventually returned to West Long Branch as a summer resident.

In the late 1800s, the intersection of Broadway and Locust Avenue was known as Lippincott's Corner. A general store and a dairy were located at this intersection.

One of the Lippincotts may have lived where the modern Lutheran church is today on Broadway, and Elisha Lippincott may have lived in the farmhouse above, according to the 1873 Beers Atlas.

At this time, West Long Branch was known as Branchburg.

In the mid-1940s, Monmouth Park was constructed in Oceanport, and this Broadway property was used as a horse farm operated by the Stingle family.

Today this building is Shore Manor, a nursing home.

The Stingle farm had a variety of outbuildings. This was the carriage house that is still standing on Pine Avenue.

Today the property has been expanded and is the private home of the Fred and Diana Boynton DeRasmo family. The Stingle's brick smokehouse can be seen at the right.

Jean Balziel (left) and her mother-in-law appear here in the late nineteenth century, as identified by the late Bella Balziel Wolcott. The house was on Broadway. It became the parish house for the Evangelical Lutheran Church of the Reformation.

Martin and Lily Lutz lived in the house in the 1920s, and Mrs. Lutz babysat local children. This photograph shows a view from the backyard. Children played in the glassed-in porch. The hound dog, Duke, belonged to Arthur Van Note, who was no immediate relation to the Cedar Avenue Van Notes.

Ella and Arthur Ambrose Van Note sold poultry and eggs from 8 Locust Avenue, which used to be occupied by the Throckmorton family. This photograph was taken in 1935.

The Van Notes' grandchildren, Ella, 11, and Herbert Arthur Jr., pose together in 1941. Ella was executive vice president of Shadow Lawn Savings & Loan; in 1992 she became its chairman. Herb was a borough policeman from 1957; he retired as captain in 1982. He married Gloria, a daughter of Daniel Dennis on Victor Avenue.

Built before 1823, 1060 Broadway stood on land that went all the way to Franklin Lake. Jacob Tallman passed it to Rebecca Tallman; the house and two acres were sold for $156 to pay his debts. Years ago it was thought to be haunted by the ghost of a boy who drowned in the Turtle Mill Brook.

This photograph of Mildred Slocum Van Brunt Hayes, 21, was taken in the early twentieth century. Millie was one of five children of William M. and Jennie Thompson Slocum. The others were Fred, a borough policeman and local fisherman; Helen, married to Long Branch banker Stanley Bouse; Joe, also a borough cop and a North Jersey oil company employee; and Mary S. Powers, who moved to California. The Slocums' prosperous 55-acre farm went to Turtle Mill Brook. Early widowed, Millie had two sons, William "Moon" and Lee Van Brunt. The latter had one child, Joyce.

Broadway at Route 36 in 1960. A Mobil station is on the far left-hand corner today, followed by Dowling Insurance. Raymond Dennis, an ice cream entrepreneur from Asbury Park, had a parlor on the next lot, followed by the back driveway and iron gates of Glenwood Cemetery. There is an office building on the right today.

Turtle Mill was built before the Revolution by Quaker patriot John Williams on the northeast side of Turtle Mill Brook. In 1868 this photograph was taken in the middle of the Red Bank-Eatontown-Long Branch Turnpike looking towards West Long Branch from Oceanport.

With dissension growing among the Independent Methodists on Monmouth Road, a faction led by Reverend Samuel Budd began in 1809 to build a church on Locust Avenue. It became the mother church of Jersey Shore Methodism from Sea Bright to Shark River, and is locally called Old First.

Though incorporated as the Methodist Episcopal Church of Long Branch, in 1939 it became The Methodist Church after the merger of the Methodist Episcopal, the Methodist Protestant, and the Methodist Episcopal South churches.

The building was finished in 1819, initially built without a spire. Interior galleries ran along both sides of the church. The pews were rough boards.

Two
Church and Cemetery

Francis Asbury, the first Methodist bishop in America, was painted by Charles Peale Polk in 1794. Methodist circuit riders have been documented in this area as far back as 1780. Asbury preached in Branchburg in 1785 (probably in William Brinley's barn) and again in 1809 while Old First was under construction. As part of his sermon, he cautioned the congregation to not make the building too small.

Old First from the Maps-Krug property, c. 1930. The cemetery surrounding the church, plus two adjoining burial yards, are now under the care of an association. Among the people who are buried here are three who were present in Ford Theater the night President Lincoln was assassinated.

The church interior shows a center pulpit, a solid, semi-circular railing, and exposed organ pipes. By 1874, the interior side galleries had been removed; in 1902 memorial, or stained-glass, windows were installed. In 1935 the Beach Memorial Chancel, dedicated to Dr. and Mrs. Beach, was installed with the new design for the altar and choir area.

The church interior is shown here in the 1995 Christmas season. The present pipes and chimes were installed in 1954, replacing ones that had been in service for thirty-eight years.

The back of the church shows the rear gallery. In 1841 the backs of the pews had been lowered, resulting in more alert parishioners during the sermon. In 1934 new pews were put in.

Locust Avenue, looking south, shows the Sunday school chapel built in 1886. Classrooms were added later. Some are now used to house the Old First Museum, which is open four times a year on Sundays and by appointment.

Old First Rectory, c. 1920, looking north up Locust Avenue.

A. Randolph "Ralph" Chinery was sexton and cemetery superintendent for fifty-four years. He died in 1942.

The New Era went down in 1854 off Deal Beach, Asbury Park, with 286 German émigrés who never made it alive to the U.S. They were buried here in a mass grave. In 1891, a group of German descent raised the money to put up a marker in their memory.

Lutherans began worshipping in the West Long Branch area in 1931, renting, among other addresses, the Junior Mechanics Hall on Monmouth Road. Reverend Carl Miller of Asbury Park oversaw the parish in 1934. In 1948 this colonial chapel was built on Broadway at Locust Avenue. West Long Branch Mayor Frank Schantz was a charter member.

On May 28, 1961, Linda Reimann, a daughter of German immigrants, and Robert Yale married in the original chapel. Flanking the bride and groom are, from left to right : Ingrid Granit, Ann Rymer Bell, William Rymer, and Thomas Granit. In 1963, Ollie Slocum & Son of West Long Branch built a modern sanctuary. The chapel became an open Sunday school auditorium. The congregation belongs to the Lutheran Church In America, organized in 1962.

Calvary Assembly of God, Broadway, was built in 1961 with boards from a building in Long Branch. The congregation had been holding cottage prayer meetings in local homes since 1928. With help from contractor Emory Polhemus, parishioners built their own church.

MAURICE PODELL
JAN. 10, 1894 · AUG. 4, 1967
ARTIST · SCULPTOR · POET

Maurice Podell's headstone appears in Monmouth Fields, one of three Hebrew cemeteries located off Broadway and North Linden Avenue. They are fronted by the non-sectarian, and older, Green Lawn Cemetery.

The Congregation Brothers of Israel Memorial Park Annex was founded by the Congregation House of Jacob and the Independent Order of Brith Araham on Laurel Street. Many individuals who subscribed to a variety of different religions found their heavenly rest in West Long Branch, where abundant farm fields were easily converted to cemeteries.

St. Jerome's Parish was created on October 18, 1956, and in June 1957 the Roman Catholic church opened its doors on Wall Street, west of Monmouth Road. Mount Carmel Cemetery on Wall Street, east of Monmouth Road, was started by Star of the Sea Roman Catholic Church in Long Branch.

"Along the beautiful and picturesque New Jersey Coast, in a sequestered spot, shaded by trees, in peaceful quiet, the paradisacal, non-sectarian Glenwood Cemetery is located, where sleep in peace the remains of those who have been borne to their last resting place." These are the dreamy introductory words from a 1925 sales brochure for a proposed mausoleum.

The reality after funds ran out. Despite this setback in the cemetery's development, a number of prominent people were still buried here. These notables include the acting duo of Charlie Ross and Mabel Fenton (who had a popular Wanamassa club) and Jacob Showles, a trained horse rider in P.T. Barnum's circus.

This view of the cemetery was taken from the highest point, looking south. Monmouth Road is on the right, and the J.H. Parker Farm is in the distance. The cemetery was pieced together from farmland owned by the Dennis and Turner families.

The other side, known locally as Cemetery Hill, is blanketed in snow every winter. The 1889 Wolverton map shows this as Dennis Hill.

Master stone cutter Ralph Ardolino Sr., from Brooklyn, bought Malchow's in 1929 and renamed it the Long Branch Monument Company. This view, c. 1930s, was taken from the cemetery at Old First, Locust Avenue, and Wall Street.

Ralph's four sons went into business with him. They are seen here with their mother and four sisters in 1947. From left to right are: (front row) Lavinia, Esther, Mrs. Caroline Ardolino, Tillie, and Jean; (back row) Daniel, Arthur, Ralph Jr., and Carl.

Office of Public Instruction

For Monmouth County,

Freehold, N. J., Dec. 6th 187?-

This certifies that Miss Virginia has our permit to teach the Mechanicsville School with the consent of the trustees, and while so engaged she shall be at liberty to exercise and enjoy all the legal functions and rights of a licensed teacher.

It being understood that this permit shall be limited to first offering presented to obtain a regular license.

Done under my hand.

[signature]

Co. S. Supt.—

Among the earliest education-related documents found in Mechanicsville is this written teacher's certificate awarded by Monmouth County to E. Virginia Croxson of Monmouth Road in 1873.

Three
Education

The first schoolhouse was built on Cedar Avenue on land owned by Elisha West in 1780. The school's next location was on Locust Avenue. In 1869-70, a two-story school was built on the northwest corner of Locust Avenue and Wall Street. Will Malchow's stone works was on the opposite corner where a gas station is now. Pictured third and fourth from the left in this photograph are Jesse Golden and Lelia Chinery. Della Golden is first on the right.

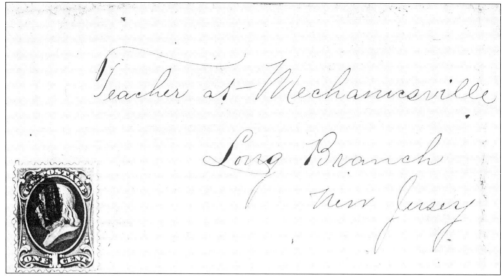

Envelope from the Monmouth County Office of Public Instruction, 1873.

This turn-of-the-century photograph features, among other students, Oliver Norton (a Bowman), Louis Palmer, William Woolley, Earl Hopper, and Lilliam (or Florence) Palmer.

The one-room Kensington Park school, near Kensington Avenue (now Rivington Street), is shown here c. 1880. A brick apartment house is on the site today.

Given the low foundation, this might have been the Locust Avenue school, and the teacher Virginia Croxson.

Those identified in this 1913 Kensington Park School photograph are Edwin Roswell (top row, second student on the right) and Beatrice Kirby (middle row, first on the right). These two students grew up to marry one another. Ida Thompson is the teacher.

In 1904 the brick grammar school was built. It was enlarged in 1914, and in 1915 the Kensington Park pupils began attending classes here. In 1908, Munroe V. Poole was appointed school district clerk; George Gibbs, school monies custodian; and Richard Hughes, representative on the board of education.

The eighth-grade graduating class of 1922 would go on to attend Chattle High School in Long Branch. From left to right are: (front row) Charles W. Dennis, Fannie Christopher, Nancy Ravashiere, and Edwin Roswell; (back row) Herbert Van Note, Raymond Bowman, Robert Tebar, Lawrance Binger, and Basil Slocum.

> This is the last will and
> testiment of the 8th grade of 1922
> To the class of 1923. We asign forever
> The 8th grade wills their books
> paper desks basket ball baseball
> and other equipments to the class
> of 1923.
> Robert Tebat wills his skill in
> pitching the pill across the pan
> to Francis Palmer.

In the class will, students appropriated their possessions and attributes to those who would follow. The document read, in part: "Lawrence Binger who is valedictorian wills his place to Arthur Hood. Basil Slocum wills his secret of winning the [affection] of all the girls to Gilson Thorne. Eddie Roswell wills his place at the dictionary looking up big words so that people may think he has a large vocabulary to Jessee Parker."

WEST LONG BRANCH
PUBLIC SCHOOL

REPORT CARD
GRADES ONE TO FIVE

PUPIL: *John Disbrow*

TEACHER: *Sara B Williams* GRADE: *4*

PRINCIPAL: *W H Ryd...* YEAR: *1942-43*

The school attempts to have all phases of its work contribute to the building of good citizenship. It is important that the home share this responsibility with the school.

The form of the West Long Branch report card has changed a great deal over the years. What has endured, however, is the borough's tradition of bringing new kindergartners together before they start school so they can get to know each other and their teachers over milk and cookies.

74

PART ONE	PART TWO
INVOCATION................*Rev. W. A. Moore*	ADDRESS
THE LORD'S PRAYER	PROFESSOR CHARLES T. STONE
CHANTED BY SCHOOL	GIRLS' CHORUSES—
CHORUS, "Stars Brightly Shining"......*Bronte*	(a) "Raining of Daffodils" *Daniel Protheroe*
SCHOOL	(b) "Our Clock"................*Edwardo Marzo*
SALUTATION	VALEDICTORY
BASIL SLOCUM	LAWRENCE BINGER
RECITATION, "The Tapestry Weavers"	PRESENTATION OF GRADUATES
NANCY RAVASCHIERI	PRESENTATION OF DIPLOMAS
SONG, "Dreams"................*Wood*	PROFESSOR CHARLES T. STONE
PRIMARY GRADUATES	PRIZES
THE CLASS PROPHECY	
written by ROBERT TEBAR	CHORUS, "Forth from Hill and Dale" *Facer*
and FANNIE CHRISTOPHER	SCHOOL
GIVEN BY HERBERT VAN NOTE	
THE CLASS WILL *written by* EDWIN ROSWELL	
and RAYMOND BOWMAN	
GIVEN BY CHARLES DENNIS	
CLASS SONG, "Down at Chattle High"	

The 1922 graduation program.

Class of 1931. From left to right are: (front row) Albert Ott, Viola Covert, Marion Townsend, Donald Johnson, Clara Woolley, Carrie Bilotta, Gaylin Malin, and Marion Huber; (middle row) William Frey, Melva Van Note, Ailene White, Grace Blakley, Principal William Hugh Ryder, Ruth Brower, Mary Shebert, Martha Peak, and Marguerite West; (back row) Howard Dangler, Eloise Hoyt, Dominic Ravaschiere, Carmela Vitaliano, John Munn, and Vera Anderson.

Boys will always be boys. These young fellows are shown catching a smoke at the garage behind the school in 1948. From left to right are: Sterling Cheek, Jerry MacGregor, John Tomaine, and Massey Odiotti. By this time, students were graduating to the new Long Branch High School on Westwood Avenue.

Class of 1949. From left to right are: (front row) Arnold Warren, Shirley Farrell, Sterling Cheek, Nancy Vieweger, Principal W.H. Ryder, Lois Brown, Jerry MacGregor, Annabelle Terwilliger, and Joan Glasser; (middle row) Frank Mathis, Mary Ann Ronan, Rheinhardt Bahrs, Ann Lewis, Steven Mathis, JoAnn Shatto, Paul Schaaff, Phyllis Kirby, and John Tomaine; (back row) Virginia Lee Dennis, Herbert Levine, Jane Walling, Jack Coates, Patricia Finn, Massey Odiotti, Carol Roswell, Raymond Kinsey, Barbara Baird, and William Thompson.

Frank Antonides Dies; West Long Branch Figure

1/26/63

WEST LONG BRANCH—Former Mayor Frank Antonides, 83, of 201 Locust Ave., died yesterday at Monmouth Medical Center, Long Branch. He was born in Tinton Falls, then Shrewsbury Township, and lived in West Long Branch most of his life.

Mr. Antonides had the distinction of being one of the two Democratic mayors in the history of West Long Branch. He served from 1923 to 1928. Before that, he was a councilman for seven years, and in 1929 was fire chief.

He was appointed to the Board of Education in 1911. The next year he was elected and served continuously for 46 years. He was secretary of the Board for 44 years.

School Named For Him

The Board of Education voted in 1958 to name the school on Locust Avenue the Frank Antonides School.

"I'm not looking for any pub-

FRANK ANTONIDES

The Locust Avenue School was built in 1951 on land farmed by Louis and Laura Lane; Frank married their daughter Nellie. The farmhouse still stands to the left of the tennis courts next to the school.

Antonides was a freight agent for the New York and Long Branch Railroad Company in 1946. He was also an exempt member of Fire Company 1, and affiliated with both the Junior Order of United American Mechanics (Norwood Council), and the Long Branch Improved Order of Red Men (Takanassee Tribe).

Ruth Dennis Wagner, seated, was a daughter of Frank Dennis. The Dennis home, with its twenty-one rooms, was worth an estimated $40,000. It was destroyed by fire on December 2, 1946. In 1959, the property was cleared to make way for Shore Regional High School, itself created to alleviate overcrowding at Long Branch High by combining students from West Long Branch, Oceanport, Monmouth Beach, and Sea Bright. The board used blueprints of a South Jersey school to save 10 percent in architect's fees.

The original section of this house was built between 1720 and 1730 by Captain Samuel Dennis. He used hand-hewn oak with mortise and peg assembly to put the beams together instead of using nails. Dennis and his son Phillip remodeled the home about 1790; Dennis's descendants remodeled it again in 1904. It overlooked Franklin Lake. At one time, the property went from Franklin Lake to Turtle Mill Brook.

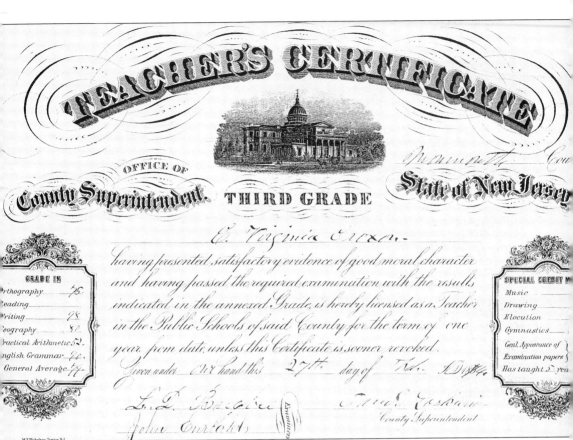

TEACHER'S CERTIFICATE

OFFICE OF
County Superintendent.
THIRD GRADE

Monmouth Cou...
State of New Jersey

E. Virginia Croxon

having presented satisfactory evidence of good moral character and having passed the required examination with the results indicated in the annexed Grade, is hereby licensed as a Teacher in the Public Schools of said County for the term of one year, from date, unless this Certificate is sooner revoked.

Given under Our hand this 27th day of Feb. A.D. 1884

GRADE IN	
Orthography	75
Reading	
Writing	98
Geography	80
Practical Arithmetic	52
English Grammar	76
General Average	79

SPECIAL CREDIT IN
Music
Drawing
Elocution
Gymnastics
Genl. Appearance of
Examination papers
Has taught 2 years

Examiner

County Superintendent

W.T. Nicholson Trenton N.J.

On the back of this certificate, county superintendent Samuel Lockwood wrote: "Miss Croxon (sic)—Please pull a little on your arithmetic. It is a pity to see that sum so low, where others are so good."

CRYSTAL SPRINGS FARM.

Long Branch, N. J., Sep, 1. 1897

M. 141 & L. 97

Bought of FRANK DENNIS,

GROWER OF ALL KINDS OF VEGETABLES

WATER CRESSES A SPECIALTY.

1897

Sep.	4	To Cash	50	Aug	20	By Bal.		21,	62
Oct,	9	" Ck	100	Sep	20	" 1 Month		75,	
"	4	" "	25	Oct	20	" 1 "		75,	
Nov	6	" Cash	10	Nov	20	" 1 "		75,	
	13	" Ck	50						

Frank M. Dennis, son of William H., started a watercress farm on the low-lying area west of Franklin Lake. Dennis also had farms in West Virginia, Maryland, and Alabama. Like many businessmen in the borough, he listed his address as the city of Long Branch. Frank's half-brother, Raymond, bought the Kurrin Ice Cream Company of Asbury Park, and had a retail store on Broadway near the Oceanport line.

Four
Merchants

Seed money totaling $1,000 launched the Shadow Lawn Building and Loan Association on the second floor of the Monmouth Road firehouse on December 27, 1927. Harry Van Note was company president. In 1940 the company received a Federal Savings and Loan Insurance Corporation insurance certificate, changed its name to Shadow Lawn Savings and Loan Association, and moved to Broadway. Assets were $1 million in 1946.

In 1948, Willis A. Woolley was president, and Shadow Lawn Savings, which took its name from Hubert Parson's Versailles-styled mansion and estate, moved to Broadway and Norwood Avenue.

Shadow Lawn Savings remodeled this corner twice. Here it is in the 1950s. By 1980, the institution had 13 branch offices in Monmouth and Ocean counties, 67,000 passbook savings customers, 8,000 mortgage customers, and $431.9 million in assets. Employees numbered 135; 45 worked in the home office.

Our Roots Go Deep
in West Long Branch

As the Borough of West Long Branch observes its Sixtieth Anniversary, Shadow Lawn Savings and Loan Association has just turned forty; old enough to reminisce yet young enough to regard the future with optimism.

When Shadow Lawn was founded in West Long Branch back in 1928; America's current hero was Charles A. Lindbergh and the Volstead Act was eight years old; you could buy a Buick sedan for $1195 and prime rib roast for 35c; W. C. Fields and Charles Conklin were appearing in "Two Flaming Youths" at the Broadway Theatre, in Long Branch . . . and our resources were $50,000.00.

As the Borough of West Long Branch has grown, this association has grown. From the modest office we opened in the Borough Hall in 1928, Shadow Lawn facilities have expanded, embracing eight offices in Monmouth County, with headquarters at Long Branch. Our current resources stand over $60,000,000.00.

To the people of West Long Branch and its governing body, we offer sincere congratulations upon this occasion. Our fond esteem and best wishes are with you as the borough enters its sixty first year.

Shadow Lawn Savings
AND LOAN ASSOCIATION

600 Broadway, at Norwood Avenue, Long Branch

| Oakhurst | Neptune City | Holmdel | Middletown |
| Keyport | Englishtown | | Middletown |

The association's 1968 advertisement in the town's 60th anniversary book. John G. Lawley was president at the time this ad was taken. In 1979, Royal E. Fliedner, an early graduate of the new four-year Monmouth College on Parson's former Shadow Lawn estate, was named president.

Ground-breaking on Joseph Bilotta's 11.5-acre farm on Monmouth and Parker Roads was the first step in the return of Shadow Lawn's headquarters to its hometown in 1981. Assets were $450 million. From left to right are: Chairman John Guire (owner of a Long Branch fuel oil firm), Director and Building Chair Charles Kitson (owner of Kitson Chevrolet, Route 36, Eatontown), President Roy Fliedner, and Mayor Henry J. Shaheen.

In 1988, the institution changed to Shadow Lawn Savings Bank, SLA. In 1990, Rochester (NY) Community Savings Bank acquired Shadow Lawn. In 1994, Sovereign Bank Corporation bought the bank and in 1995 sold the building to Jersey Shore Medical Center.

This sign is one of the few artifacts that remains from William J. Bridge's dairy-processing operation at 971 Broadway. From 1926 to 1940, Bill and his son, Ralph, sold raw and pasteurized milk, cream, and cottage cheese. Mr. Teicher bought the dairy operation, moved it to Long Branch, and renamed it Woodside Dairy.

The American Silk Mills Company, 804 Broadway at Oakwood Avenue, was part of a $2 million enterprise with factories in several states. This location employed four hundred at its peak. Its original location was a small plant with fifty employees on Division Street in Long Branch.

Milton Rubin owned the American Silk Mills. At this plant raw silk was spun into thread and then into bolts of fabric like crepe de chine, satin, and georgette. Passersby on Broadway could hear the looms clacking all day and all night.

The fabric was turned into ladies' underwear, pajamas, coat and suit linings, mufflers, shirts, and even Air Force parachutes. The majority of the employees were women, some of Italian and Polish descendent. Some were young girls from Shamokin and Philadelphia who came during the Depression, when the mills where they worked closed. Some were also local children as young as twelve. An expert mill worker could handle four looms at one time, and was paid $25 a week. In 1933 the National Recovery Administration—in an effort to end the Depression— passed the National Industrial Recovery Act. The act established minimum wages, maximum hours, and collective bargaining. It also abolished child labor. Franklin D. Roosevelt was president.

That same year, Philo Farnsworth developed electronic television. New York won the World Series against Washington. George Balanchine and Lincoln Kirstein founded the School of American Ballet. Robert Byrd led his second expedition to the South Pole. George Cukor directed *Dinner At Eight*. James Joyce's *Ulysses* was allowed into the U.S. following a court

AMERICAN SILK MILLS INC.

NRA
MEMBER

WE DO OUR
AMERICAN

N.R.A. Parade Long Branch Nov. 1 1933

ruling. Humorist and short-story writer Ring Lardner died.

The boycott of Jews began in Germany. Mass starvation in the U.S.S.R. reached disastrous proportions. The Nazis erected the first concentration camps. And, Adolf Hitler was granted dictatorial powers.

Archibald Gathers managed this factory. One day in the late 1930s, Gathers came to work, took out a gun, and shot himself to death in his office. No one knows why. But some retired employees say the U.S. government found defects in the mill's parachutes.

Rubin closed the factory, offering his employees the chance to move to Orange, VA, where he had another silk mill. Some went. Many of those with families stayed. They came back to work here in 1940 for Lewis Seitzman. The Newark entrepreneur had a factory on Branchport Avenue, Long Branch (where Wheelock's is now), but eventually moved into the bigger mill space when his orders for military uniforms increased.

In the 1950s, Seitzman took on a partner and the business acquired a new name—Robert Lewis, Incorporated. The company made heavy men's outerwear for J.C. Penny, Ward's, and Sears. In the 1960s, it moved further into retail. By 1980, Lincoln, Seitzman's son, sold his family's share of the business. The building now houses car and paper inventory.

The 1873 Beers Atlas shows the Kensington Park neighborhood north of Broadway. Park Avenue became Victor Avenue, and Kensington became Rivington. Park Place became Windsor Avenue, and Windsor Terrace does not exist today. Oakwood Avenue is the side street coming along the L. Dreyfus property, facing J. Beebe's lot on Broadway. In 1904 Oakwood was part of the dividing line between Long Branch City and West Long Branch.

Ar right, Barbara and Joseph Sacco celebrate their 50th wedding anniversary in 1961. Barbara worked in the silk mill and Joe built houses in the area, including two on Mitchell Terrace in West Long Branch.

The American Silk Mills baseball team is shown below. In 1938 they were photographed at Flanagan Field on Atlantic Avenue in Long Branch. From left to right are: (front row) Nappi Ulrich and Les Wilcox (who came to work in the mill to earn tuition money for Cornell. He later went to work for Fort Monmouth, and was a councilman in 1984.); (back row) Warren Wilcox, Mr. Farmer, Paul Greco, "Puppy" Rusigno, Frank Christopher, "Skinny" Wike, Willie Tomaino, and Anthony "Tote" Christopher.

Like other merchants, Kirby used Long Branch as his business address. It is possible his mail was also delivered through the city.

The Christopher siblings from Kensington Park. The children are identified from left to right, and their occupations or places of residence are listed in parentheses. Front row: Helen Grasso (Fort Monmouth), Bessie Barbieri (real estate), Fannie Dorsey (California), Rose Olivadotti (president, local International Ladies Garment Workers Union), and Mary; (back row) Anthony (EAI), Paul (Fisher's Bakery), Frank (plumber), Greg (plumber), and Dominic (NJ Tobacco).

In 1913 William Dennis, son of William and Martha Dennis of Long Branch (and no relation to Frank Dennis), partnered with Samuel Peak in a mill that finished wood for interiors. Daughter Marion married Joe Bilotta's son, Frank, who became police chief. From left to right on Victor Avenue in the 1950s are: (front row) Rob Peak, Marty Drahoes, and Joe Giglio; (back row) son Daniel, Mort Thorne, Anthony Juliano (?), and Joe Flavin. Becker's Tree Service is on the mill site.

Broadway and Oceanport Avenue's northeast corner was the site of a beer-bottling works. The first owner was James Randolph in 1893, and he was followed by John Alberto and Joseph Fiorillo. Robert Wholstrom was the last owner of this enterprise, because the newly-formed West Long Branch Borough Council outlawed this industry in 1908.

Paul DeFilippo, born 1892 in Italy, had a cinder and concrete company in Long Branch until ill health forced him into another line of work. In 1932 DeFilippo built a grocery store on farmland newly zoned for commercial use. He set the building on an angle because of a plan to push Maple Avenue through to Wall Street. The store opened March 20, 1933. In January 1934 he moved his family from Long Branch. His wife Angelina looks out from the second-floor window.

The building from Larchwood Avenue. Just beyond the lattice work, DeFilippo tried out a restaurant where, for a year, he served what could have been Monmouth County's first pizza. After Paul died in 1940, Angelina and their oldest daughter, Rosemary, ran the business until Anthony, their young son, turned twenty-five.

Rosemary married Domenic Nannini, an Oceanport butcher, in March 1946. When they returned from their honeymoon, they bought the grocery store from Angelina.

A year after the repeal of Prohibition in 1933, DeFilippo obtained a liquor license. In 1938 he opened this bar on the other side of the grocery store. It is now an office behind the retail liquor store. The current bar is located between the liquor and grocery stores.

ELECTRONIC ASSOCIATES, INC.
LONG BRANCH, NEW JERSEY

WORLD LEADER IN ANALOG COMPUTING, PLOTTING, RECORDING,
AND CONTROL INSTRUMENTATION EQUIPMENT

1945 - 1958

CHRONOLOGY OF GROWTH

October 31, 1945	—Incorporated in the State of New Jersey as Electronic Associates, Inc.
November, 1947	—Operations expanded into present North Long Branch plant.
July, 1954	—First fully equipped Analog Computation Center in the United States starts operations in Princeton, New Jersey.
April, 1955	—New Sales Office opened near Chicago, Illinois.
January, 1956	—Additional Manufacturing space acquired on West Avenue in Long Branch.
September 1, 1956	—New Sales Office opened in Los Angeles, California.
November, 1956	—Fully equipped Computation Center opened in Los Angeles, California.
March, 1957	—Digital Computer Computation Facility opened at Princeton Computation Center.
April, 1957	—European Regional Office opened in Brussels, Belgium.
July, 1957	—Third Computation Center starts operations in Brussels, Belgium.
August, 1957	—Construction started on new manufacturing plant in West Long Branch.
March, 1958	—Electronic Associates, Inc. chosen to represent U.S. Analog Computing and Plotting Industry at the 1958 World's Fair in Brussels, Belgium.
March, 1958	—Southwestern Regional Office opens in Dallas, Texas.
May, 1958	—First operations start move into nearly finished West Long Branch manufacturing Plant.

EAI on Route 36 was dedicated November 1958 on what had been a corn field for the Flock Farm, and before that, the Covert Farm. From left to right are: Lea Adamson (vice president and co-founder), Mayor Owen Woolley, and Lloyd Christianson (president and co-founder).

Charlie Maps, an engineering graduate of the Stevens Institute of Technology in Hoboken, poses in his office in the 1980s.

The EAI building today is used as an office complex by a variety of corporations.

Angelo Valenzano came to the Jersey Shore from Jersey City in 1959 and opened a stationery store on the ground floor of apartments built by Frank Krug. In 1964 he opened the new store on Locust Avenue. In 1975 he was a borough councilman.

Elizabeth Virginia Croxson, born in 1840 and independent like her mother, Rebecca Cox, would also raise a daughter single-handedly. Virginia's father may have been from Oceanport.

Bertha Croxson is shown here as a young woman. In 1922, the state took 22 feet off Monmouth Road to widen Route 71 and paid the Croxson women $200.

By the 1920s the Croxson house had a second floor. Eventually Bertha would be the second wife of Frank S. Brand, one of the borough's original councilmen. They had no children.

Croxson Corner, as it could have been called, was the scene of a "Hatfield-and-McCoys'" animosity between two highly independent widowed farm women each waiting for the other to die in order to buy the remaining property. Emma Golden eventually died first of injuries sustained when a car hit her in Ocean Grove.

Charlie and Emma Golden Parker owned what was the Goodrich Farm in the swale of land just north of the Croxson homestead, where the four-lane highway of Route 36 is today. In 1900 they called it Sunshine Farm.

When the state put in Route 36, Emma had her roadside stand moved close enough to Bertha's for the two women to spend the rest of their days squabbling over the property line. Emma lived in a lean-to added to the back of the stand.

The Sunshine Farm Stand was in the green triangle of land at the Monmouth Road cut-off from Route 36. Freeholder Fred A. Beale lived in this house across Monmouth Road, and had a little fish market out front. His father, John, had owned the farm where K-Mart and the Mews at Turtle Mill is today. His heirs sold it to the Muccio family.

The Charles M. and Lydia Anne Parker Homestead on Parker Road later became a dump and is now Home Depot. The couple had five children: John H., James, George, Ella, and Charles (who married Emma Golden). John and James worked together in New York as contractors and builders. John became president of the National Realty Corporation and of the Corduroy Pulp and Lumber Company in Newfoundland. He retired in 1919. His first wife was Kate Edgeley.

John Hubbard Parker's fancy house was located on Monmouth and Parker Roads, west. With his second wife, Jennie, he had two children, John H. Jr., and Esther Maud. Jennie lived here until she died; she was well known for her philanthropy and was a founder of the Methodist Episcopal Home for the Aged in Ocean Grove. She lost her legs in a train accident, and was chauffeured everywhere.

The Turner Brothers Nursery on Monmouth Road was owned by Turner brothers Artie and Ernie, who lived side by side on the northeast corner of Parker Road. In the early 1970s, Jack Harakal bought the business, and the name changed to Frank's. Cappy Pearce, who worked with the brothers, bought their landscaping business, which still uses the Turner name. This photograph was taken in April 1958.

When The Occasion Demands The Finest

The following are but a few of our many personalized suggestions.

FIRST — A COCKTAIL PARTY @ $2.50 PER PERSON FOR ONE HOUR. Preceding the dinner reception a never-ending flow of tempting appetizing and delectable hot hors d'Oeuvres and Canapes, and also a never-ending flow of Manhattans, Daiquiris, Martinis, and Whiskey Sours.

APPETIZERS: Jumbo Shrimp Cocktail +50c.
Antipasto +40c.

PASTA: One Manicotti or Ziti Macaroni with Bolognese Sauce. If the Pasta is substituted for Soup +25c. If served as a separate course +40c.

ENTREES: Roast Shell Sirloin Steak Bordelaise Sauce +$2.00.

Roast Prime Ribs of Beef +90c.

Rock Cornish Hen Stuffed with Wild Rice +$1.00.

Prime Sirloin Steak with Mushroom Cap +$2.00.

Prime Filet Mignon with Sliced Mushrooms +$2.50.

Boneless Breast of Capon, Stuffed with Wild Rice +$1.25.

ASSORTED COOKIES

From

OUR OWN BAKERY

per tray $2.00

Joseph's
FESTIVE FRUIT TABLE
The Masterpiece of
Delectables +90c

Listed above are the bridal menu choices available at Joseph's for the wedding reception of Rosemary Soltis and Sterling Cheek Jr. on December 26, 1966. Joseph, his wife Victoria, and mother-in-law first worked in this country for Louis B. Tim, a Manhattan shirt-maker whose estate was on Westwood and Bath Avenues in Long Branch. Joseph was the butler, Victoria was Mrs. Tim's maid, and "Maman" was the cook.

102

Tory and Ida Kawamoto had a restaurant on Broadway and Ocean Avenue in Long Branch when Tory bought a farmhouse on Monmouth Road from C.E. Anderson in the early 1930s. He converted it to a restaurant, creating a fish pond with a waterfall in the front garden. Tory's was a popular place when Ida fell ill at the outbreak of America's involvement in World War II. When the military came to put Tory in an internment camp, Kawamoto hanged himself outside E.C. Hazard's hospital in Long Branch. Ida died a year later in 1943. Both are buried in Glenwood.

The Belgian-born Joseph Dammon (shown at right) bought the restaurant after owning the Norwood Hunting Lodge on Locust Avenue and working at the Jumping Brook Country Club in Neptune.

Joseph's appears here as most remember it. One remaining driveway jockey holding a lantern graces the driveway of Rosemary and Sterling Cheek's home on Whale Pond Road in West Long Branch. Today, Squire's Pub is owned by Basil Plasteras.

Bertha Croxson was a secretary for Frank Dennis, traveling with him to various produce farms. She and her mother were avid letter-writers. In one correspondence, Virginia thanks Bertha for sending Swiss chard, but mentions that there was so much she fed what was left over to the cats.

Besides selling watercress, Dennis was also the ice man, cutting his ice from Franklin Lake where Lakeview Avenue is today. After a long, hot, dry spell when the water level drops, you can see the foundation's outline. This photograph was taken *c.* 1900.

Thomas Eagen, left, and Ralph Ardolino Sr. pose in 1935 on the front steps of the house Ardolino built for his family next to his stone-cutting business. Born in Italy in 1869, Ardolino worked on the Lincoln Memorial. Locally, some of his best work is found in the Woodbine Cemetery in Oceanport.

Fire Company No. 1 is lined up at the intersection of Monmouth Road and Cedar Avenue at Christmas-time c. 1940.

COMMUNITY CHRISTMAS SING
Borough of West Long Branch
Sunday Afternoon, December 21, 1947
at 5:00 o'clock

The tree has been in many locations, from Chester Dennis's front yard on Wall Street, to the intersection of Monmouth Road and Cedar and Locust Avenues, to the front of the Community Center. When he was a councilman, Realtor Anthony Camassa donated the tree that now stands permanently in Woolley Park. West Long Branch may have been the first Monmouth County community to start the civic tradition of lighting a tree in 1916.

Five
Community

In 1876, the U.S. mail to greater Long Branch was delivered first to East Long Branch, the postal designation of the lower village nearest the shore. West Long Branch's mail was delivered from Long Branch City, or the upper village, at Branchport and Norwood Avenues.

On June 29, 1957, Leon Cordner relocated from the Long Branch Post Office to West Long Branch, bringing with him Mail Route No. 3 that covered Oceanport Avenue, Broadway, and Norwood Avenue. This move finally consolidated all the borough's mail in one post office.

From left to right in front of the borough's post office at 587 Cedar Avenue in 1959 are: Bill Conway, John Pittenger, Andy Frees, Ed Marino, Ruth Brower DeBruin (George Gibbs's niece), Nick Mancini, Ray Shuda, and Leon Cordner.

John Pittenger appears on Locust Avenue with the bicycle he used to deliver the afternoon residential mail. A GM Chevy truck was used for the morning run to curbside mailboxes.

One of the borough's earliest public works trucks, shown below, was used to wet down the dusty dirt roads.

Franklin Lake Park is seen here from Locust Avenue *c*. 1940. Not only had the lake been deep enough at one time to provide blocks of ice, but it also was thick enough for ice-skating parties.

The parkland around the lake is used to commemorate highlights in the borough's history. This is one of the millstones from Turtle Mill that was excavated by the West Long Branch Historical Society before a parking lot was paved over the site.

TESTIMONIAL

Dinner

and

Reception

Given in Honor of

"Chet" Bowman

with the hearty co-operation
of the
NORWOOD GOLF CLUB
at its Club House

August 13, 1924

by

"The Home Folks," former Chattle
Classmates and a host of admiring
friends from all over Monmouth
who are justly proud of his many

Chester Bowman graduated in 1921 from Chattle High School, where he excelled in track and football. At Syracuse University he was a fullback and also played basketball, but it was in track and field that he distinguished himself. In 1924, he went to the Olympics in Paris, where he helped set a gold-medal record of 41 seconds in the 400-meter relay. Bowman was also largely responsible for setting up the first community Christmas tree at the intersection of Monmouth Road and Cedar Avenue. Sadly, Bowman took his own life in 1936 at age thirty-five.

Golden's store is divided between a barber shop and Bill's Food Market. The Maps-Krug House is in the background. Come late afternoon, traffic would be rerouted as residents filled the intersection to sing carols. Borough electrician Chester Dennis did the lights. This photograph was taken *c.* 1940.

By this time McGregor's colonial inn was being used as an apartment house. Later it would be a tea room. The Beach-Woolley House is at left. The Christmas song list included a Unison Reading and a Pledge of Good Will and Love Toward All.

In 1902, Eatontown Township helped establish its third fire department with a steel-frame truck equipped with chemical tanks and ladders. The men pulled this apparatus until 1915, when the company bought a pair of fire horses from the Neptune Fire Company of Asbury Park for $350.

West Long Branch Fire Company No. 1 appears here *c.* 1920. From left to right are: Russ Hagerman Jr., Louis Huhn, Dutch Norton, Ralph Huhn, Solomon Sherman, Allen Woolley, Herbert North, Francis Golden, Henry Schultz, Dave Svenson, Vincent Kublin, Harry Dennis, unknown, and Chester Dennis. The driver is Russ Hagerman Sr.

From left to right in this picture are: (front row) Ollie Norton, Tom Monahan, Charlie Stillwagon, Harry Brower, Louis Huhn, Art Van Note, Harry Hopper, Stan Johnson, Jim Atcheson, Roy Bowman, and Reg Van Note; (middle row) Allan Woolley, Beverly Brown, Ralph Chinery, Frank Dennis, Walt Sherman, Frank Antonides, Brick Woolley, and Gene Magee; (back row) Sol Sherman, Dick Cooper, Langdon Norton, Norm Poole, John Heyer, and Fred Worles. Ralph Huhn is the little boy in front.

The Home of
Fashion Park Clothes
SHOES AND FURNISHINGS

LEON A. WOOLLEY
183 B'WAY   LONG BRANCH

PROGRAMME

1—OPENING CHORUS—"Medley" - Entire Chorus
    Introduction of Stillwagon and Atcheson
    Introduction of Van Note and Bowman
2—"Dear Heart" - - - - - Norman Poole
3—"Take Your Girlie to the Movies" - "Brimm" Bowman
4—"The New Moon" - - - - Bertha Edwards
    Introduction of Norton and Woolley
5—"I've Got My Captain Working For Me Now"
                     "Charley" Stillwagon
6—"Medley" - - - Woolley Brothers Quartette
7—"How Ya Gonna Keep 'Em Down on the Farm?"
                     "Jim" Atcheson
8—"Tell Me" - - - - - Howard Poole
9—"Alexander's Band" - - - "Shorty" Norton
10—"Toy Land" - - - - Allan R. Woolley
11—"Alabama Lullaby" (Duet) Marion Clark-Grace Atcheson
12—"Oh What a Pal Was Mary" - - "Brick" Woolley
13—"Oh Lawdy" - - - - "Reg" Van Note
14—CLOSING CHORUS - - - Entire Company

The minstrel show, held November 28, 1919, in the Sunday school chapel of Old First, was used to raise money for a modern fire truck.

Company No. 1 is lined up in front of Owen Woolley's house on Wall Street. From left to right are: Charlie and Mickey Huhn, Bobby Van Note, Bill Antonides, Harry Dennis, and three unknown persons. Dickie Wilson is the young boy riding with Santa Claus, whose real identity is also unknown.

Company No. 2 is gathered in front of Cora Dangler's Rae Shoppe, Hair Dresser of Fashion, located on Broadway near North Linden Avenue. "Hat" Woods is the first on the right. In 1915 William Dennis spearheaded the effort to create a local fire department; one year later, West Long Branch Fire Company No. 2 was inaugurated.

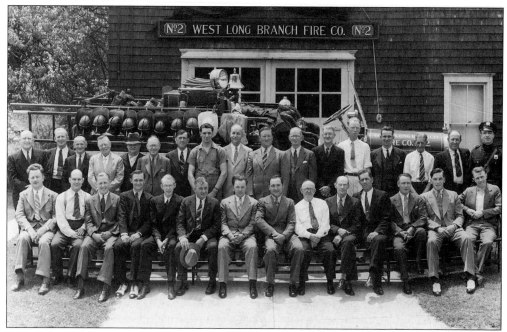

From left to right are: (front row) John Rohbeck, Dan Dennis, Herman Rohbeck, Howard Kirby, Chas. Morgan, John Tibbitt, Geo. Conway, Moon Van Brunt, Harry Wood, Bill Dennis, Marshall West, Geo. Wood, John Conway, and Chas. Brower; (back row) Bill Morgan, J. Price Hood, Sam Peak, John Davison, Bob Parker, Halsey Phelan, Chas. Schlentz, Tony Cosentino, Harry Clerk, Edgar "Fat" Howland, Henry Schultz, Mort Thorne, Gil Thorne, Ed Roswell, Al Frey, and Frank Bilotta.

In February 1959 a fire broke out at the sixteen-lane West Long Branch Bowling Alley on Broadway and Golf Street. The Mack pumper supplied water for six continuous hours.

NYCFD's fireboats tour, in the early 1980s. From left to right are: Steven Fitzpatrick, unknown, Charlie Cook, Tony Riddle, Michael Thorne, Kevin Fitzpatrick, and Ron Fitzpatrick. Thorne became a firefighter for company 2, but lost his life putting out a fire at Monmouth College. The park at the end of West Campbell Avenue is named in his memory.

The police department was established in 1908 with two marshals. In the 1920s, a motorcycle patrolman, Robert Hoyt, covered the borough; a much thinner Hoyt than the one we know today is pictured above. It was a two-man operation until 1954, when the department expanded to match the town's suburban and commercial development.

116

Charter Members
of the
WEST LONG BRANCH FIRST AID SQUAD

Raymond Antonides, Raymond Bowman, Roy Bowman, Charles Brower, Harry Cooper, Chester Dennis, Harry Dennis, Albert Fry, Edgar Howland, Robert Hoyt, Clarence Morris, Francis Palmer, Raymond Poole, John Tibbets, Calvin Woolley.

The squad was organized in April 1931. In August 1955, it bought a fully-equipped Cadillac ambulance.

Welcome Home Dinner

Tendered by

The Mayor and Members of the Borough Council
of West Long Branch

In Honor of

THE MEMBERS OF THE FIRE DEPARTMENT
AND THE FIRST AID SQUAD
OF OUR BOROUGH
WHO SERVED IN WORLD WAR II

JOSEPH'S RESTAURANT
MONMOUTH ROAD

Tuesday Evening, April 9, 1946
AT 7:00 O'CLOCK

Civic pride is one of the chief traits of the West Long Branch community. Here is an example of that pride as it related to the war.

Below is an example of how rationing worked during the war.

UNITED STATES OF AMERICA
War Ration Book One

WARNING

1 Punishments ranging as high as *Ten Years' Imprisonment or $10,000 Fine, or Both*, may be imposed under United States Statutes for violations thereof arising out of infractions of Rationing Orders and Regulations.

2 This book must not be transferred. It must be held and used only by or on behalf of the person to whom it has been issued, and anyone presenting it thereby represents to the Office of Price Administration, an agency of the United States Government, that it is being so held and so used. For any misuse of this book it may be taken from the holder by the Office of Price Administration.

3 In the event either of the departure from the United States of the person to whom this book is issued, or his or her death, the book must be surrendered in accordance with the Regulations.

4 Any person finding a lost book must deliver it promptly to the nearest Ration Board.

N°: 611529 —343

August 16th /(5

Camp Davis near alandria "Va

Dear Cousin,

I received a letter from
you some time ago, I was in Washington
at the time I was very glad to here from
you but wasant that awfull that affare
of abby Slocum to think that she should
be shot by her own husban. I cant
hardly think that Peter ever shot her but
it's hard to tell what they wont do at these
times you said in your letter that you
wood write soon again or I wood of written
before now I am in the State of Va
again we left washington 14th & it
is awfull drye whether here is very unhellthy
once in a great while we have a little
shower dont mount to much & water
is very scarce here to allthough we are

This letter was written to Virginia Croxson by her cousin Gardner from Camp Davis, VA, where he was stationed with New Jersey's fourteenth regiment in the Civil War. The first page registers shock at the news that Abby Slocum was murdered by her husband, Pete. Pete apparently preferred his wife's sister, Alcine Chasey. Gardner's letter doesn't reveal any fear related to the war, but he does urge his cousin to write him frequently.

In 1958 West Long Branch celebrated its 50th anniversary, and some of the anniversary committee members are shown here. From left to right are: (front row) Mrs. Edwin Berger, Nina Klein, Mrs. Orville McClain, and Fran Townsend; (middle row) John Disbrow, Harvey Leuin, Bob Megaro, and Andy Kromi; (back row) Howard Kirby, Harry DeCamp, Harry Cooper, and Vincent Kublin.

Merchants set up displays in the Community Center. Domenic and Rosemary Nannini recreated their Wall Street grocery store. Louise Errico (Kinsey) was Miss West Long Branch. The Nannini daughters are Caroline (top), Angela (left), and Rita.

Harry Cooper, Louise Errico, and Dick Cooper show off the display for Cooper's Service Station, which was then selling Sunoco products.

The Community Center was decorated for the anniversary celebration. The monument in the center commemorates residents who gave their lives in World War II.

The Cedar Sportsmen's Club was started in 1952. On April 30, 1955, the group held a Junior Sportsman Show at the Community Center. Elizabeth Deming and Ivan Wordin were first-prize winners in the birdhouse-building contest. MC for the show was John Disbrow, club secretary, who also handed out the awards.

In 1983 the borough celebrated its 75th anniversary. Some of the committee members stand with a Gannett Outdoor employee in front of a Route 36 billboard promoting the anniversary. From left to right are: the Gannett representative, Anthony Sgro, Mayor "Clint" Sorrentino, and John DeBruin. An important date in the mayor's life is also important to the community of West Long Branch: his birthday—June 22—is also the anniversary of the borough's first council meeting.

The Sherman-Gibbs store on Monmouth Road became the College Park Cleaners; its second floor was the long-time meeting room of the Junior Mechanics fraternal order.

Awards ceremony for Pack 45. In the rear from left to right are: Ray Russomano, Howard Woolley (a Long Branch clothier), Frank Christopher, Vern Bennett, Frank Woolley, unknown, Sidney Johnson, unknown, County Sheriff Paul Kiernan, and Tom "Ducky" Delisa. On the far left in the front row is Stan Buff, in the center is scout Dick Disbrow, and to the far right is Joe Welsch.

First officers of the Lion's Club. From left to right are: (front row) Dominick Bizzarro (lumberyard manager), Tom Cooper (fuel oil company owner), Bill Morgan (insurance salesman), Joe Caruso (lumberyard owner/architect), and Willard Conover (luncheonette owner); (back row) Howard Noble (advertising agent), Eddie DeSantis (garage owner), Charles Morgan (lawyer; son to Bill), Joe Dammon (owner of Joseph's), George Penterman (dairy rep), and Harry DeCamp (insurance adjuster).

At the 25th anniversary of the West Long Branch Community Center in 1979 are, from left to right: Harvey Leuin, Fred Metler, Harry DeCamp, and Charles Morgan. The Community Center was founded by the Lion's Club.

124

Police Chief Bob Hoyt, Mayor Jim Mount, Borough Magistrate Harvey Leuin, and Fireman Charlie Brower stand alongside the firehouse in the 1930s. Monmouth Road is in the background.

On June 2, 1971, a park was named after the late Russ Woolley where the McGregor House once stood. The town bought the property from the estate of Asbury Park resident Harriet M. Wilkerson for $17,000. The house was torn down in 1967. From left to right are: J. Russell Jr., Virginia W. Riley, Governor William T. Cahill, and Mayor Henry J. Shaheen.

Top left: Janet Woolley Tucci dances with her grandfather, J. Russell Woolley Sr., at her wedding in 1966. In 1984 she became the first woman elected to the borough council. Top right: Richard Cooper and son, Dick, age 1, pose together in 1935 at the Cooper House on Monmouth Road. The Fulton House is behind them. Richard and Dick followed the political path to council set by Thomas Cooper Sr.

The West Long Branch Borough Council in 1987 was notable not only because two of its members came from well-known political families, but also because for the first time in the town's history it included an Italian-American mayor. Shown here from left to right are: (front row) Ralph Yamello, Mayor Frank Sorrentino, and Janet Tucci; (back row) Anthony DeLauro, Dick Cooper, John Paolantonio, and John Kolibas. Sorrentino, Tucci, and Cooper continue to serve on the council in 1996.

Acknowledgments

For their unflagging enthusiasm, and their willingness and readiness to open old trunks, family albums, the pages of history, and beloved and trusted memories, and to patiently answer my never-ending round of questions, I would like to thank the following people.

Thomas Bazley and the West Long Branch Historical Society (who helped with pp. 11, 15, 23, 23, 24-27, 30-32, 52, 60-61, 71, 75, 78, 101, 104, 111, 114, 116); Marion Dennis Bilotta; Howard and Gertrude Poole Bradley; Jennie Cosentino Breglia; Joyce Van Brunt Caffyn (p. 54); Anthony, Camassa, and Annie Norris Carbone; Freida Larson Chasey; Karen Chateaux; Sterling and Rosemary Soltis Cheek (pp. 62, 76, 102); and Keith Christopher (pp. 16 and 90).

Mary Vespery Christopher; Alexander Cosentino; Richard Cooper (pp. 13-14, 105, 121, 126); and John and Ruth Brower DeBruin and the Old First Methodist Church Museum (pp. 17, 36, 39, 57-59, 106, 118, 122-123).

Chester "Chetty" Dennis; Diana Boynton DeRasmo (p. 51); Raymond and Ruth Disbrow (pp. 40-43, 74, 122); and the people at Dorn's Photo, Red Bank—Kathy Dorn Severini, Jeannette G. Massas, Ed Ostrander, and especially John Pecyna.

Elsalyn Palmisano Drucker (pp. 17-22); Milton Edelman (p. 123); Royal Fliedner (pp. 81 and 84); Arthur and Nancy Van Note Herry (pp. 28-30, 110, 113); Mickey Huhn; Dolly Franco Iamello (pp. 15-16, 67, 105); and Charlie Maps (pp. 9-10, 12, 14, 15-16, 23-26, 28, 31, 36-39, 45-47, 54-56, 60-61, 65-66, 69, 70-72, 91, 95, 108-109, 112-113, 124, 126.)

Fred and Frances Townsend Martinson; James C. Migliaccio (pp. 115-116); George H. Moss Jr.; Rosemary DeFilippo Nannini (pp. 92-93, 120); Doris Van Huel Orendorf; Greg Pearce (p. 101); John Pittenger (pp. 107-108); Elizabeth Canolco Ravaschieri; Virginia Woolley Golden Riley (pp. 34-35, 63-64, 125); Edwin Roswell III (pp. 70, 72-73); Mary and Vincent "Blackie" Sacco (p. 89); and Frank Scatuorchio, who helped kick the ball down the hill.

John and Shirley Mount Schmitt (pp. 68, 70, 79, 80, 96-100, 104, 119); Lincoln Seitzman; Beverly Taylor Smith; Janet Woolley Tucci (pp. 11, 32-33, 126); Ann Valenzano (p. 96); and Glenn D. Vogel (pp. 85, 91), my Eatontown book partner who happily took me through snow-covered cemeteries in his truck.

Ella Van Note West (pp. 52, 53, 82-84, 121, 124), who came along at the right time with enormous perseverance to help fill in many of the blanks ; Ira White; Les Wilcox (pp. 86-89); and Linda Reimann Yale (p. 62) who, along with her sister Ann, and nephew, Kyle Rymer (Ann's son), also helped feed past, present, and no doubt future, research and writing projects.

Bibliography

The Early History of West Long Branch, C.H. Maps and R.F. Van Benthuysen, 1977; *The Township of Ocean Centennial Commemorative Book*, 1949; *Entertaining a Nation: The Career of Long Branch*, WPA, 1940; *Old First United Methodist Church: A History of the Jersey Shore's Oldest United Methodist Church Erected in 1809*, Reverend Robert B. Steelman, 1984; *History of Monmouth County, 1664-1920*, Volumes I, II, III, 1922; *Monmouth County Police Chief Association 50th Anniversary Book*, 1990; *Asbury Park Sunday Press*, July 15, 1962; *Asbury Park Press*, September 15, 1967.

This 1965 aerial shows how some of the country estates in West Long Branch have changed. The first dormitories for Monmouth College went up around Nevesta Lee, the former home of Leopold and Eva Stern. Their home would be first owned by Highland Manor School for Girls and Junior College and then by Monmouth College. Rosedale was owned by William Henderson, then by stage actors John W. Albaugh and Mary Lomax Mitchell, then by Joe Miller, and finally, as Marlu Farm, was owned by Maurice and Lucile Pollak, who left it to Monmouth College. Shadow Lawn, the one-time John McCall estate, became Hubert Parson's lavish home just before the stock market crashed. His mansion is now called Wilson Hall and houses most of the administrative offices and some classrooms of Monmouth University.